Colonial Spanish "Horse of the Americas"
For Kids

I0440810

Nature Books for Kids
By
K. Bennett

Mendon Cottage Books

JD-Biz Publishing

Read More Amazing Animal Books

Purchase at Amazon.com

Table of Contents

Introduction

Author Bio

Introduction

Feeling down? Saddle up. *~Author Unknown*

***

Colonial Spanish: The Colonial Spanish horse is a very special horse. Do you know why? Because it's more than one horse!

What does "more than one horse" mean?

The term "Colonial Spanish" is a group of horses with different names. Names like:

*Spanish mustang
*Crillo horse
*Chilean horse
*Peruvian Paso
*Abaco Barb
*Iberian Sulphur horse
*Sulphur mustang

These horses came from Spain to the Americas and their ancestor is the Iberian horse.

The Iberian Horse

Iberian horses are native to the Iberian Peninsula. This means they come from this area.
What is a Peninsula?

The dictionary describes a Peninsula as: '*A piece of land almost surrounded by water or "coming" out of a body of water.*' The Iberian Peninsula is on the southwest part of the European continent. If you would like to see it on a map, ask your parent or a guardian to help you search.

Colonial Spanish Horse

These beautiful horses have an old history. Before they were known as Colonial Spanish horses, they were called "Jennet or Spanish Barb." There are just a few unique Colonial Spanish horses left, so this breed is in danger of extinction.

How big are they?

The size can be large or small. Some are between 13 – 14.2 hands and some stand at 15 hands or more.

Where do Colonial Spanish horses come from?

These beautiful horses came to the New World (Americas) with the Spanish explorers many years ago. Then they started to grow and multiply and soon they spread all over the country.

The website **Livestockconservancy.org** notes: "*Spanish horses were the most common type of horse throughout the Southeast and all of the regions west of the Mississippi.*"

That means at one time, these horses were the most common type of horse you could find!

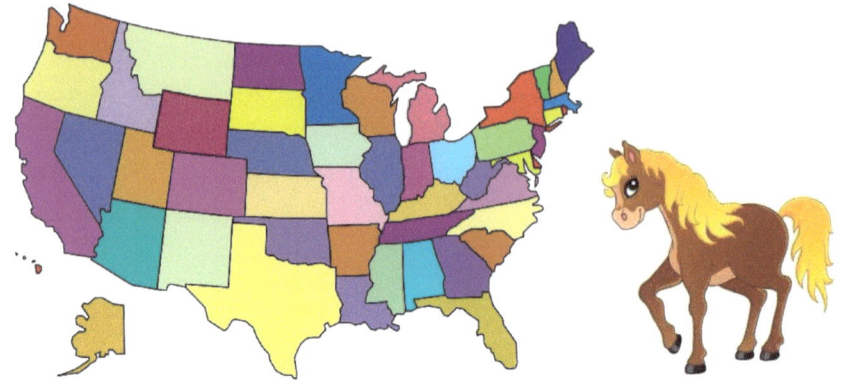

The Colonial Spanish breed is an amazing horse. For one thing, this breed is actually Spanish! So it has a good name. They have good energy too, so the horse is great for different disciplines, endurance competitions and riding. (Keep reading for more information on this subject).

What makes this horse special?

The Colonial Spanish horse has amazing colors like black, bay, sorrel, palomino and cream. And exotic coats like zebra dun, red dun, champagne and silver dapple. But wait! We're not done yet.

Many of the base colors combine with patches or white hairs on the horse. What happens then? Unique designs like paint, leopard complex, roans and more!

With their amazing colors, gentle personality and rich ancestry, the Colonial Spanish is an amazing horse to learn about. I hope you take a moment to read a little more about this beautiful animal and share what you learn with others!

HOW TO DRAW A SIMPLE HORSE FOR KIDS:

Would you like to learn how to draw a horse? Wikihow.com has a simple, but neat tutorial. Here are the steps to get started:

1- First, ask your parent's or a guardian's permission to go online.

2- In your browser (Chrome, Internet explorer, Firefox, Torch) type: www.Wikihow.com

3- In the search box at the top of the page type: *Draw a simple horse*. Once the search is complete, you should see a title that reads: "**How to draw a simple horse: 11 steps with pictures**."

4 – Click on the link and follow the steps.

5- Have fun!

Chapter 1

Hi, it's nice to meet you!

History: To understand where this beautiful horse came from, we have to go back in history to the time of the Conquistadores! Do you remember who they are?

Who were Spanish Conquistadores?

They were Spanish warriors with good skills on the battlefield. Many had military fighting skills and could use weapons very well. Others were good at teaching and being community leaders.

As warriors, they needed something to help them fight. After all, there were no cars, trucks, airplanes, submarines or tanks back then. Can you guess what the Conquistadores used to help them on the battlefield? Yes! Horses. Horses like the Colonial Spanish breed.

The Golden Age of Spain

This was a time when everything was going great in Spain, especially in the artistic department! That is why it is called the Golden Age. The Colonial Spanish horse is a descendant of the horses during this time period. This is why this beautiful creature is so important in history. **Livestockconservancy.org** calls them a *"treasure chest of genetic wealth."* This means we can learn a lot about their history if we look into their past!

What makes these horses so special?

The Spanish had a lot of success with this horse in the New World, and the Colonial Spanish spread in many places. Some of the horses also escaped and ran away! Out in the wild, they roamed freely across the plains. These became wild herds in the North American region.

However, after a while the horses were mixed with other horses like: Thoroughbreds, Tennessee walking horse, draft horses and other riding breeds. How did this happen?

Well, many of the wild herds got a little too close to ranchers or the Calvary riders. Then the horses were caught and crossed with other horses. When the baby horses were born, they were trained for military or ranching purposes.

This type of behavior is called Crossbreeding. Do you know what this word means?

The dictionary at Kids.Net.Au defines this word like this: *"(genetics) the act of mixing different species or varieties of animals or plants and thus to produce hybrids."*

So they mixed the horses together to make a new horse!

Sadly, by the 1950's, the Colonial Spanish breed was almost extinct.

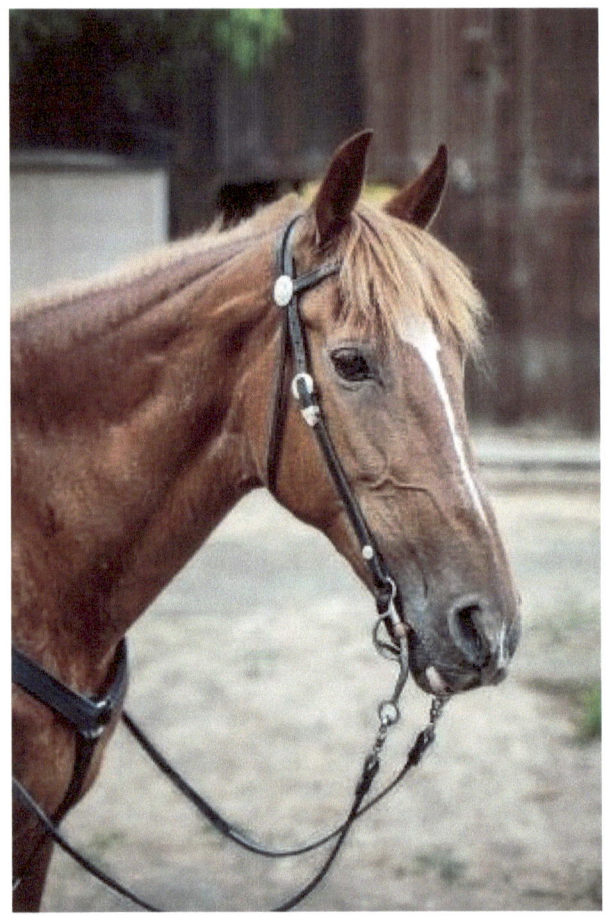

But it's not all bad news! After the 1950's, when only a few purebred horses remained, dedicated groups started to work hard to save them! Many conservation programs began dedicated to saving the Colonial Spanish breed. Programs like:

*The Spanish Mustang Registry
*American Indian Horse Registry
*Spanish Barb Breeders Association
*Southwest Spanish Mustang association

The efforts by these breeders helped to protect the Colonial Spanish breed and give them a chance to survive. Isn't that wonderful news?

FUN FACTS FOR KIDS: Measuring horses: What is **HANDS**?

This is a neat way to measure horses. The measurement refers to hands, literal hands!

Many years ago, people did not have rulers or measuring sticks like we do today. So they used whatever they had…and they had hands. So horses are measured in hands. You can do this too! One hand is 4 inches.

So if a horse is 15 hands multiply this by 4. (15 x 4) and you will get 60 inches. And if a horse is 16 hands multiply this number by 4. (16 x 4) and you will get 64 inches.

Now that you know how to do it, you can measure the other horses for yourself. Have fun!

This grass is yummier!

Strengths: Colonial Spanish horses are tough little creatures, but they have a heart of gold. They are great on rugged hillsides and mountains. They also love to be around people, so that makes them a really nice horse to have around.

For many years, this horse was called a Spanish Mustang and many people still use that name. But an article by *D. Phillip Sponenberg, DVM, PhD from Virginia-Maryland Regional College of Veterinary Medicine* changed things. How?

He said these horses are not really Spanish mustangs because *"many of them never had a feral background."* This means the horses did not originally come from feral horses.

What is a feral horse?

This horse is usually called a "wild horse." It roams freely but it wasn't born that way. It comes from domesticated horses that were owned by someone. Usually, these horses escaped their owners and ended up living "in the wild."

Why is the Colonial Spanish different?

Remember: They were brought to the New World by the Spanish conquistadores as a purebred Spanish horse. So what makes them different is their "origins."

Yes, it is true that some feral horses were included in the group but they were not Colonial Spanish. They were just another group of horse that came along.

Weaknesses: Sadly, there are not many of these beautiful animals left despite the heroic efforts of those who are trying to save them. So if you want to get one, it might be a little hard to find the "right" one.

CURIOUS FACT FOR KIDS:

An article written at *Stablemanagement.com* dated August 31, 2014 has a really neat article with the title: *"Spanish Treasures Found in Arizona: Cruce Colonial Spanish Horses."*

It talks about a lady by the name of Ms. Wilbur-Cruce. She donated 77 Spanish horses to the American Minor Breeds conservatory. You may wonder: What's so special about that?

Well, these horses were pure bloods! That is verrryyyyyyy hard to find today. So how is this possible? If you want to know more, ask your parent or a guardian to help you research this information.

You may decide to use this story for show and tell or as a school project!

Relaxing on the soft sand

Characteristics: As we talked about in the beginning, Colonial Spanish horses can be big or small.

Height: Approximately 14 hands. Most are 13 to 14.2 hands. Those who are exceptional will be 15 hands or a bit more.

Weight: 700-800 pounds. Some may weigh a little more but this is the usual weight.

Stride: Usually, a very long stride.

Gait: Single foot, pace, running walk, etc.

Meaning of terms: *A stride* means to: walk with very long steps. And **gait** means: a particular way or walking.

When you walk, do you walk differently sometimes? A horse does too! **Coats:** Colonial Spanish horses have beautiful coat colors like black, bay, sorrel, palomino and cream. Champagne is also a beautiful color and Roan. Have you ever heard of this color before?

Roan: This is not just one color. It is a pattern of colors with a mixture of white. The horse will have lots of white hairs mixed with their other hairs. Usually the head, lower legs, mane and tail are more solid or will have fewer white hairs. Sometimes, this color variation is called Silvery.

Beautiful coat

Training: Training a Colonial Spanish horse is in many ways like training other horse breeds. So let us detail the steps for training all horses to give you a better idea.

Wikihow recommends the following steps:

1-**First of all, don't scare the horse**. That means you should not run up or sneak up on them suddenly. This is not a hard to understand. For example, do you like it when people run or sneak up on you suddenly? It may scare you when someone does that, right? Then a horse will feel the same way.

2-**Be gentle and talk gently to your horse**. There is no need to yell, shout or talk in a harsh tone to your horse. Again, this idea is not hard to understand. Do you like it when people talk to you gently? Or do you want them to shout and yell at you? Isn't it nicer to treat others kindly and don't you appreciate it when others do the same for you? Your horse will appreciate your kind manner too!

3-**Most horses love to be touched**. Show them your feelings through your hands. Stroke them on the head, massage their neck, hug them, brush them and communicate your affection through gentle fingers. Imagine how happy your horse will be!

4-**Try to spend as much time as you can with your horse**. In any friendship, regular visits are the key! No matter what you have to do, stop by and visit your horse just to remind them that you're there. They will be so happy to see you and the more you spend time with them, the stronger your bond will grow.

5- **A nice reward**. A tasty treat, rub or pat down, yummy food, grooming of whatever other treat you might have in mind, will be a great idea! Do this at the end of the day to let your horse know how much you enjoyed spending time with them.

Royalgrovestables.blogspot.com notes another beautiful attitude of horses. It is their intuition or intuitive nature. This means a horse can **sense** your feelings, emotions and will react on those feelings.

If you are angry, upset, unhappy or grouchy, the horse will sense these negative emotions. This will not help you to get close to them. Instead, they may avoid you. But if you are positive, upbeat and happy to be around them, they will feel this as well. This will draw them to you and you will be able to bond with them!

Chapter 2

Just getting a bite to eat!

Have you learned anything new about the Colonial Spanish horse? Wonderful! But there is still a little bit more we can learn about them.

Because of their amazing abilities, Colonial Spanish horses are used in many disciplines, endurance competitions and riding skills.

Skills like Gymkhana, barrel racing, speed and racing events. What are those?

Gymkhana: This equestrian event (for horses) is speed pattern racing and timed games for riders and their horses. If you have never heard of this word before, not to worry! I think the Native American word is better to understand. They call this type of games "O-Mok-See," which means: "games on horseback."

This means a horse and rider play games together! This show is for many people to enjoy and the horse and rider get points for good horsemanship.

It is not only for adults. Kids get to participate too! Would you like to try? How much you learn and how fast you go is up to you.

Barrel racing: This type of show has a pattern. A clover leaf pattern. Do you know what a clover leaf is?

Think about this scene…

The arena is clear…everything nice and clean. 3 barrels are placed in 3 different places. All of a sudden you hear the go and a rider comes at full speed! Vaaaa-rroooommmmmm!!! They go as fast as they can near the barrels without tipping them over. If you tip the barrel you lose points, but if you leave them standing, you gain points.

How long should this take? Well, you have 60 seconds for the event and it depends on the arena, space and more…but the winning speed should be around 13 to 14 seconds!

How long is that? Count one Mississippi, two Mississippi, three Mississippi, four Mississippi…and when you get to 14 stop. There! That's how long it would take. Can you ride fast like that?

The winner is the fastest rider so you have to beat the clock to get the prize.

Don't forget you don't just ride in a straight line…remember the clover? Yes! It's a pattern, so you have to respect it and ride in three different directions. Think of a triangle and you will get the idea.

On your mark…

Get set….

Go!

Wild and Free!

Colonial Spanish Horses teach us a lot about the horses that used to run freely in the wild. If you would like to learn more about them, get a parent or guardian to help you research.

Here is something to help you get started: If you are a fan of scientific topics, then go to this website: *Arkwild.org.* It talks about the Wild Horses of Abaco. An article dated Feb 25, 2014 talks about the last (and yes, you read right) Abaco horse named Nunki: He is the last Abaco Spanish Colonial Horse. What happened to him? Look it up and find out!

CURIOUS FACT FOR KIDS:

Horses, like us, have different titles for different stages of life. For example when a horse is born until 6 months of age it is called a *foal*.

Then up to the age of 2 years it is called a *yearling*. If the horse is a male horse it is called a *colt* under the age of 4. When it is older than 4 years it is called a *stallion*. Do you remember what a Stallion is?

Meaning of Terms:

A **stallion** is a: Male horse that can have kids.

A **gelding** is a: Male horse that cannot have kids. (Geldings are usually patient, calm, quiet and well behaved.)

A young female horse or pony is called **filly** and after the age of 4, she is called a **mare**. (Source: **Lessonpaths.com**)

Chapter 3

Here are a few additional facts about horses in general you may like to know. (Source: ***Onekind.org***)

-A horse can express its emotions in many different ways. It can use its face, eyes and ears to tell you how it feels!

-Horses are great at keeping watch. It is rare to see a herd with everyone snoozing at one time. There is usually one horse standing as a lookout, and his job is to warn the others if danger comes near!

- Avoid standing behind a horse. They have great vision, but there are a couple of blind spots. Can you guess what the back part of the horse is? Yes! It's a blind spot. If the horse gets angry or scared, guess what he might do if you stand directly behind him?

-Horses are great at listening! They can turn their ears in different ways to improve their hearing. If you whisper and say something bad about your horse, they just might hear you!

- Horses can help people get better when they have mental or health problems. This is called: ***Equine Assisted Therapy***.

-Horses are the best sleepers on the planet. They can sleep lying down and standing up! Can you do that?

- Horses are herbivores. Do you know that this means? It means they eat plants or are plant eaters, if you like this term better.

Love you too!

GENERAL HORSE TIPS FOR KIDS:

If you are able to get a horse, you will need to care for it. So here are some tips you can think about. These basic principles apply to most if not all horses. (Source: Frank Bell- *Horsewhisperer.com*)

-Your horse's diet is very important. Some horses have very hot blood and some have cooler blood. If your horse is hot blooded, they will need less protein in their diet. Shires are cold blooded.

-Learn how to properly discipline your horse. Remember: These animals are very sensitive. Let them know when they are getting too out of control! This can be done with a shhhhh noise or a firm tone to let them know who is in control.

-If the horse's head is high it means your horse is not relaxed. They may be upset in some way. If their head if low they are relaxed. Try to get your horse to stay relaxed. This will help them feel good and both of you will enjoy the ride.

-Horses love to get your tender rubs and soft pats. Things like rubbing their ears, nose, eyes and mouth is great. And a massage is even better!

-If a horse is trained really well, he or she will invite YOU for a ride. You should be looking for the invitation! Then you will enjoy an awesome ride.

-Your horse can sense your moods and behavior. If you are confident your horse will be confident too!

-You should feed your horse from a bucket and not your hand. (This is the recommendation, but I feel it is better to feed them with your hand from time to time! It seems to generate more trust and respect, but that is just my humble opinion on the subject. What do you think?)

INTERESTING FACT FOR KIDS

Do you know the scientific name for horses? They are called Equines which comes from the Latin word meaning Equus Caballus. Can you think of any other creature that looks like a horse? Did you think of a donkey? Maybe a Zebra? What about a mule? These are also related to the Equus Caballus.

Horses can live for many years. Some for 30 years and in some cases 40 years or more! Ponies can live for a very long time too. But if you want to know how old they are you need to look into the horse's mouth! Have you heard of this practice before? Usually the approximate age of a horse is estimated based on the incisors, upper and lower in the mouth. What is that? The teeth!

Can you tell how old you are by looking at your teeth? (Source: *Lessonpaths.com*)

Conclusion

In conclusion: Horses are beautiful creatures, and Colonial Spanish horses are no exception. This energetic, fun loving and good natured horse is a wonderful example of how amazing Earth's creatures can be.

They have a "free" spirit but they are willing to work hard. They are happy to be a part of your life and with a little love and affection, your bond will grow for years to come.

This is a great time to learn a bit more about these noble animals. You may be amazed at what you can discover. If you don't know where to look, ask your teacher, a parent or guardian to help you. They may have some great ideas too!

If you don't know exactly what to research about this noble breed, then think about this: Why don't you choose something you really like (It can be the tail, mane, ears, body, size, personality, history, etc) and learn a bit more about that particular subject?

If you are in school and you participate in show and tell, use that as your subject. Many of your classmates may not even know what a Colonial Horse is really like, so it would be nice to share what you find with others!

I hope this book has taught you just how wonderful nature is and how each creature can impact our life in amazing ways.

Colonial Spanish Horses are a special part of nature's magnificent wonders!

Author Bio

K. Bennett loves to write for both children and adults. Many different subjects are interesting to develop, but writing for children is special to her heart.

Her favorite pastimes include reading, traveling and discovering new things. Each of these activities helps to fuel her imagination and acts like a blank canvas waiting for more stories.

She is intrigued with fantasy elements like hidden worlds and faraway lands. Basically anything that gets her imagination soaring to new heights!

Her writing credits include children books online, short stories for online magazines, and two novellas listed at Amazon.com

Our books are available at
1. Amazon.com
2. Barnes and Noble
3. Itunes
4. Kobo
5. Smashwords
6. Google Play Books

Publisher

JD-Biz Corp

P O Box 374

Mendon, Utah 84325

http://www.jd-biz.com/

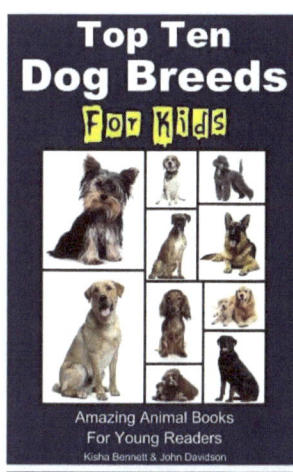

Top Ten Dog Breeds For Kids
Amazing Animal Books For Young Readers
Kisha Bennett & John Davidson

Poodles
Dog Books for Kids
K. Bennett

Labrador Retrievers
Dog Books for Kids
K. Bennett

German Shepherds
Dog Books for Kids
K. Bennett

Rottweilers
Dog Books for Kids
K. Bennett

Boxers
Dog Books for Kids
K. Bennett

Golden Retrievers
Dog Books for Kids
K. Bennett

Beagles

Dog Books for Kids
K. Bennett

Yorkies
Dog Books for Kids
K. Bennett

www.ingramcontent.com/pod-product-compliance
Lightning Source LLC
Chambersburg PA
CBHW040317010626
45792CB00023B/820